The YouTube Shorts
Mastering the Art of Getting Likes

Introduction

The rise of YouTube Shorts has transformed the digital landscape, revolutionizing how content is created and consumed. With short-form video gaining immense popularity, YouTube Shorts has emerged as a powerful platform for creators to engage with audiences in innovative ways. These bite-sized videos, lasting 60 seconds or less, have taken the world by storm, offering a unique opportunity for content creators to showcase their creativity and build an audience rapidly.

In today's fast-paced digital world, mastering Shorts is no longer optional – it's key to standing out and achieving success. Whether you're a seasoned content creator or just starting, understanding the nuances of Shorts is essential to stay relevant and tap into the ever-growing audience that seeks quick, engaging, and easily digestible content. The potential for viral success, increased visibility, and audience growth is higher than ever for creators who can produce captivating Shorts.

This book will guide you through the process of creating compelling YouTube Shorts that not only capture attention but also attract likes, shares, and subscribers. We'll explore the best practices, tips, and strategies that will empower you to craft Shorts that resonate with your audience, boost engagement, and enhance your overall content strategy.

IDEA 1: Understanding the YouTube Shorts Ecosystem

What are YouTube Shorts?

YouTube Shorts are short-form, vertical videos that can last up to 60 seconds, designed specifically for mobile consumption. They are a part of YouTube's effort to compete with other platforms like TikTok and Instagram Reels, offering creators a unique format to share quick, engaging content. Shorts can feature everything from trends, challenges, and tutorials, to snippets of longer videos, all aimed at grabbing attention in a matter of seconds. The format leverages YouTube's powerful algorithms to surface content to users based on their interests, making it easier for creators to reach a broader audience.

The Power of Short-Form Video Content

Short-form video content has proven to be incredibly effective in capturing and maintaining the attention of viewers in a world increasingly dominated by fast consumption habits. With smartphones becoming the primary device for media consumption, and social media users scrolling rapidly through their feeds, short videos allow creators to deliver their message or entertainment quickly and effectively. This format is ideal for connecting with younger audiences, who prefer content that's easily consumable and shareable. Furthermore, the rise of platforms like TikTok and Instagram has solidified short-form video as a dominant trend in the digital content space.

Key Differences Between Shorts and Traditional YouTube Videos

While traditional YouTube videos can range from a few minutes to several hours, Shorts are designed to be quick, punchy, and attention-grabbing. Here are the key differences:

- **Length**: Traditional YouTube videos can vary widely in length, but Shorts are capped at 60 seconds. This shorter format encourages creators to focus on delivering content in a concise and impactful way.
- **Orientation**: Shorts are vertically formatted, optimized for mobile viewing, while traditional YouTube videos are usually horizontal (landscape) and cater to both desktop and mobile users.
- **Engagement**: YouTube Shorts is centered around quick discovery and engagement. Users can swipe through Shorts similar to how they interact with other platforms, like TikTok, creating a more spontaneous interaction with content. On the other hand, traditional videos on YouTube often

rely on search algorithms or subscription feeds.

- **Monetization**: Traditional YouTube videos are eligible for monetization through ads, sponsorships, and other revenue streams. While Shorts can generate ad revenue as part of the broader YouTube monetization strategy, the focus is more on building a community and driving engagement.

Understanding these differences is crucial to harnessing the full potential of YouTube Shorts and tailoring your content to the platform's unique ecosystem.

How the YouTube Algorithm Promotes Shorts

The YouTube algorithm plays a crucial role in determining which content gets seen by users, and understanding how it promotes Shorts can help creators maximize their visibility and engagement. Here's a breakdown of how the algorithm works for YouTube Shorts:

1. **Discovery Through the Shorts Shelf** YouTube's algorithm surfaces Shorts through the **Shorts shelf**, a dedicated section within the app where users can swipe through a stream of vertical videos. This feed is designed for quick

consumption, making it easier for users to discover content that matches their interests. The algorithm curates this feed based on a combination of factors, including user behavior, engagement patterns, and content relevance.

2. **User Behavior and Engagement**
One of the most significant factors in the algorithm is how users interact with content. Metrics such as:

   o **Watch time**: The total amount of time a viewer spends watching a Short. Higher watch time indicates that users find the content engaging.

   o **Likes, comments, and shares**: These interactions signal to YouTube that viewers find the content valuable, which can increase the likelihood of that Short being recommended to others.

   o **Replays**: If users watch the video multiple times, this signals strong engagement, prompting the algorithm to prioritize the video for wider visibility.

3. **Personalization**
YouTube's algorithm personalizes recommendations based on a user's viewing history, subscriptions, and interactions. For Shorts, this means that the content is tailored to users' preferences, even if they've

never seen a particular creator's video before. The more a viewer engages with certain types of content (for example, comedy, tutorials, or travel), the more the algorithm will push similar content to them.

4. **Relevance to Trends**
   YouTube is highly influenced by trending topics, challenges, and viral content. Shorts that align with popular trends or utilize trending music and hashtags have a higher chance of being featured to a larger audience. This helps creators tap into larger conversations and expand their reach.

5. **Consistency and Frequency**
   Creators who post frequently are often rewarded by the algorithm. YouTube tends to favor channels that consistently upload Shorts, as it indicates an active presence on the platform. Consistency helps build an audience over time, as frequent uploads give the algorithm more opportunities to test which content resonates with users.

6. **Title, Description, and Hashtags**
   Although YouTube Shorts don't require detailed descriptions, creators can still use titles and hashtags to give context to the content. Hashtags, in particular, can help the algorithm categorize the content, making it easier to surface in relevant searches or feeds. By strategically using keywords related to the video's topic or

current trends, creators can improve their visibility.

7. **Watch History and Recommendations**
The more someone watches Shorts, the more likely YouTube will recommend similar content. If a viewer frequently engages with food-related videos, for instance, the algorithm will push more food-related Shorts to their feed, even if they don't follow a particular creator. As a creator, appealing to a specific niche or interest can increase the likelihood of your Shorts being recommended to a targeted audience.

8. **Diverse Content Styles**
The YouTube algorithm also promotes diverse types of content. Whether it's humor, educational content, or storytelling, YouTube is constantly experimenting with new content types. Creators who innovate with unique, high-quality Shorts that stand out can benefit from increased exposure, especially if their content catches the algorithm's attention for being new or different.

In summary, the YouTube algorithm promotes Shorts by focusing on user engagement, watch time, consistency, relevance to trends, and personalization. By understanding these factors, creators can tailor their content to be more discoverable, ultimately attracting a larger audience and increasing their chances of going viral.

IDEA 2: Setting Up for Success

Choosing Your Niche: What Resonates with Your Audience?

One of the most important steps to succeed with YouTube Shorts is identifying a niche that resonates with both you and your target audience. By narrowing your focus, you can create content that appeals to a specific group of viewers, helping you build a loyal following. Here's how to choose the right niche:

- **Assess Your Passions and Expertise**: Think about what you love to create or talk about. Whether it's humor, tutorials, fitness, fashion, or travel, your niche should align with your interests and skills, allowing you to produce content consistently and authentically.
- **Understand Your Audience**: Conduct research into what's popular within the Shorts ecosystem and who your target audience is. What do they care about? What

problems can you solve for them? Understanding their preferences will guide your content strategy.

- **Research Popular Trends**: Look for content that's trending within your chosen niche. Use YouTube's Trending section and explore other platforms like Instagram Reels and TikTok for inspiration. Pay attention to the style, topics, and format of successful videos in your niche.
- **Create Content for a Specific Purpose**: Is your content meant to entertain, educate, or inspire? Aligning your content with a clear purpose will help it stand out and increase its chances of being shared.

By focusing on a niche, you can refine your content, develop a recognizable brand, and attract a dedicated audience that shares your interests.

Optimizing Your Channel for Shorts: Thumbnails, Descriptions, and Tags

Even though YouTube Shorts are quick, bite-sized videos, it's still essential to optimize your channel and individual videos for maximum reach and engagement. Here's how to do it:

- **Thumbnails**: While YouTube Shorts often play automatically in the Shorts feed without thumbnails, when your Shorts appear in other places (like search results or recommended videos), thumbnails still matter. Create eye-catching thumbnails that complement the video's content, even if the video is short. Use bright colors, bold text, and clear imagery that stands out in both small and larger views.

- **Titles and Descriptions**:
  - **Titles**: Keep them concise and compelling. The title should give viewers a reason to click on the video while accurately describing the content. Include keywords that people are likely to search for, but avoid clickbait.
  - **Descriptions**: Though not as crucial as in traditional YouTube videos, a good description can still help your video appear in search results and provide context. Use it to briefly explain what the Short is about and include any relevant links, hashtags, or calls to action.
- **Tags**: Use relevant tags to categorize your Shorts and help YouTube understand the content. Tags should be specific to your niche, video topic, and popular search terms. Although tags aren't the only factor in discoverability, they still play an important role in matching your content with users' interests.

- **Hashtags**: Including hashtags in your video title or description helps YouTube categorize your Shorts and can boost their discoverability. Make sure the hashtags are relevant to your video's content. Using trending hashtags can also increase your chances of being featured on the Shorts shelf.

Essential Tools and Equipment for Creating High-Quality Content

To create compelling YouTube Shorts that stand out, investing in the right tools and equipment is key. Here's a list of essential gear for producing high-quality content:

1. **Smartphone or Camera**: Since YouTube Shorts are typically vertical videos, a smartphone with a good camera is usually sufficient. Modern smartphones, especially iPhones and Androids, offer high-quality video recording capabilities. If you prefer using a dedicated camera, ensure it can shoot in 4K resolution and has a good autofocus system.
2. **Stabilization Tools**:
   - **Tripods**: A tripod ensures steady shots. Some are adjustable to different heights, while portable

tripods are useful for filming on the go.

- o **Gimbals**: For smoother, more dynamic shots, a gimbal can stabilize your phone or camera while you move. This is especially important if you plan to shoot fast-paced, action-packed content.

3. **Lighting**:
   - o **Ring Lights**: Great for even, soft lighting that minimizes shadows and enhances your appearance. Ideal for beauty or tutorial content.
   - o **Softbox Lights**: These provide diffused light and are perfect for shooting indoors or in dim lighting.
   - o **LED Panels**: Adjustable and portable, LED lights are great for adding creativity and controlling lighting effects in your Shorts.

4. **Microphone**:
   - o **Lavalier Mic**: A clip-on microphone that provides clear audio for talking-head videos or tutorials.
   - o **Shotgun Microphone**: For directional audio pickup, especially useful if you're filming in a noisy environment.
   - o **Bluetooth or Wireless Microphone**: These are great for filming on the

move or when you want to avoid tangled wires.

5. **Editing Software**:
   - ○ **Mobile Apps**: For quick editing, apps like InShot, Adobe Premiere Rush, and CapCut are user-friendly and perfect for mobile creators.
   - ○ **Desktop Software**: If you're creating more advanced edits, consider software like Adobe Premiere Pro or Final Cut Pro for better control over your footage, effects, and transitions.

6. **Props and Backdrops**:
   - ○ **Simple Backdrops**: A clean background or creative backdrop can elevate your video. Consider using neutral or thematic backgrounds based on your niche.
   - ○ **Props**: Depending on your content, props can add visual interest or help demonstrate a product or concept more effectively.

7. **Post-Production Tools**:
   - ○ **Royalty-Free Music**: YouTube's music library or other platforms like Epidemic Sound or Artlist offer tracks that can be used in Shorts without copyright issues.
   - ○ **Graphics and Animations**: Use animated text, stickers, or other graphic elements to make your

Shorts more engaging. Tools like Canva or Adobe After Effects can help you design custom animations.

By setting up your channel, optimizing your content, and using the right equipment, you'll be better prepared to create high-quality YouTube Shorts that resonate with your audience, stand out in the feed, and keep viewers coming back for more.

IDEA 3: Crafting the Perfect Short

The 3-Second Hook: Capturing Attention Immediately

In the world of YouTube Shorts, where viewers' attention spans are incredibly short, the first few seconds of your video are critical. You have just **3 seconds** to grab their attention before they decide whether to keep watching or swipe to the next video. Crafting a strong hook is essential for keeping viewers engaged. Here's how to do it:

- **Start with Intrigue**: Begin with something that sparks curiosity or creates a sense of mystery. For instance, you could ask an engaging question, showcase an unusual or unexpected visual, or provide a teaser of something exciting that will happen later in the video.

- **Present the Problem**: If your video is educational or a tutorial, quickly introduce the problem you'll solve. For example, "Struggling with productivity? Here's a quick tip that will change your day!"
- **Visually Captivating**: Use striking visuals right away—this could be an interesting prop, a burst of color, or an exciting action. People are more likely to stop scrolling if something visually appealing or unusual catches their eye.
- **Dynamic Movement**: Movement is engaging, especially in short-form content. Starting your video with quick action, such as a jump cut, a product reveal, or something dynamic, can immediately captivate the viewer's attention.

The goal is to hook your viewer in the first few moments by offering them something they want to know or see, ensuring they stay engaged throughout the 60 seconds.

Building Emotional Resonance: Humor, Inspiration, or Surprise

Once you've captured attention with your hook, you need to maintain it by building emotional resonance. The most successful Shorts evoke a strong emotional response from the viewer, whether through humor, inspiration, or surprise. Here's how to incorporate these elements:

- **Humor**: Humor is one of the most effective ways to engage viewers. A funny moment or punchline can create a positive emotional connection, encourage sharing, and build your audience. Whether it's a witty one-liner, an exaggerated reaction, or a clever twist on a popular trend, humor is universally appealing. Remember to keep it light and relatable, and avoid going overboard so that it feels genuine.
  - o **Tip**: Use facial expressions, timing, and editing to enhance the comedic impact. A well-timed pause or reaction can make all the difference.
- **Inspiration**: People turn to YouTube for motivation and inspiration. Whether it's fitness progress, personal growth, or stories of overcoming challenges, inspiring content leaves viewers feeling uplifted. Creating a narrative that empowers or motivates will resonate with audiences who appreciate positivity.
  - o **Tip**: Share a personal story, a positive affirmation, or a relatable struggle that leads to triumph. Keep the tone

optimistic and ensure the message is clear by the end of the Short.

- **Surprise**: Surprise is a powerful tool in keeping your audience engaged. A twist in the narrative, an unexpected revelation, or a dramatic reveal can make your content memorable. Whether it's a shocking fact, an impressive transformation, or an unforeseen outcome, surprise keeps viewers hooked and makes your video stand out in a crowded feed.

  o **Tip**: Build up anticipation and then deliver something unexpected. This can be a plot twist, a funny moment, or even a surprise challenge. The element of surprise will encourage viewers to share your video or come back for more.

Balancing the Emotional Elements

You don't have to choose just one emotional element—sometimes, combining humor, surprise, and inspiration in a single Short can create a dynamic, engaging video that appeals to a wide range of emotions. The key is to balance these elements so that they feel natural and not forced. For example, you could start with a humorous moment, lead into an inspirational message, and then end with a surprise twist.

Call to Action (CTA)

Although the primary goal of your Short is to entertain or inform, a well-crafted CTA can guide your viewers toward further engagement. After establishing emotional resonance, gently prompt your viewers to like, comment, or share the video. You can even encourage them to check out your other content or subscribe for more. Keep the CTA simple and unobtrusive so that it doesn't disrupt the flow of your video.

Crafting the perfect YouTube Short involves capturing attention with a strong hook in the first 3 seconds and then building emotional resonance with humor, inspiration, or surprise. By combining these elements effectively, you can create Shorts that not only entertain but also leave a lasting impression on your audience.

Ending with Impact: Encouraging Engagement Through Likes and Shares

To make your YouTube Shorts truly effective, it's important to not only capture attention and evoke emotions but also to **encourage engagement**. Ending your Shorts with a compelling call-to-action (CTA) can motivate your viewers to like, comment, share, and subscribe, all of which increase the likelihood of your content being promoted by the YouTube algorithm. Here's how you can end your video with impact:

- **Clear, Direct Call to Action**: After delivering your content, directly ask viewers to engage. Whether it's "Like this video if you agree!" or "Share this with a friend who needs to see this!" being direct helps give the viewer a clear next step.
  - ○ **Example**: "If this made you laugh, hit that like button and share it with someone who needs a smile today!"
- **Engage Through Comments**: Ask a question in your video or encourage viewers to share their thoughts in the comments. This not only boosts engagement but also helps create a sense of community around your content.
  - ○ **Example**: "What would you do in this situation? Let me know in the comments!"
- **Use Interactive Elements**: If appropriate, use interactive features like polls or challenges in your Shorts. This gives viewers a reason to interact with your content beyond just watching.
  - ○ **Example**: "What's your favorite trick? Comment below and I might feature your idea in the next video!"
- **Reminder to Subscribe**: In Shorts, where video lengths are short, a reminder to

subscribe can work wonders if done at the right time. Place it towards the end but not in a way that feels forced or too salesy.

- o **Example**: "Want more tips like this? Hit that subscribe button and stay tuned for more!"

- **Leave Them Wanting More**: To inspire shares, you can tease upcoming content, hint at a new video series, or create a sense of anticipation.
  - o **Example**: "Don't miss the next video—where I'll be showing you the next crazy hack! Subscribe and hit the bell so you're the first to see it!"

By ending your video with a clear CTA, you encourage your audience to interact with the video, which can lead to more views, shares, and likes, ultimately boosting your presence on the platform.

Examples of Successful Shorts with Analysis

Looking at successful Shorts can provide insight into what works and why. Here are a few examples, along with an analysis of why they're effective:

1. **Example 1: Viral Dance Challenge**

- What Happened: A simple, catchy dance to a trending song was posted, with the creator adding their own twist (such as funny facial expressions or unique moves).
- Analysis: This Short succeeded because:
    - Trending Music: Using a song that's trending ensures the video gets picked up by the algorithm and recommended to viewers interested in that song.
    - Relatable Content: Dance challenges are fun and easy to engage with. People love recreating these moves, leading to shares and likes.
    - Emotional Resonance: The humor and creativity added to the dance make it more memorable, increasing the chance of the viewer sharing it with others.
    - Call to Action: "Tag someone who needs to try this challenge!" encourages interaction.

2. **Example 2: Funny Pet Moment**
   - What Happened: A dog attempts a trick but fails in an amusing way,

accompanied by humorous commentary.

- o **Analysis**: This Short was successful because:
  - **Universal Appeal**: Pets are loved by many, and funny pet videos tend to get shared widely across social media.
  - **Timing and Editing**: Quick cuts and comedic timing emphasize the funny moment, keeping the audience engaged throughout.
  - **Viewer Connection**: The humor makes it relatable—viewers who own pets can identify with the situation, making it more likely to be shared with others.
  - **Call to Action**: "Does your pet do this too? Comment below!" creates a direct invitation for viewers to engage with the content.

3. **Example 3: Quick DIY Hack**
   - o **What Happened**: A fast-paced tutorial on a simple life hack, such as how to fold a shirt in 2 seconds.
   - o **Analysis**: The video worked because:
     - **Valuable Content**: People love learning something new,

especially when it's quick and easy to apply. The practical nature of the video encourages viewers to share the hack with others.

- **Short and Sweet**: The video delivers immediate value without dragging on, perfect for the quick-consumption nature of Shorts.
- **Surprise**: The unexpected simplicity of the hack creates a "wow" moment, increasing the likelihood of the viewer sharing it to impress others.
- **Call to Action**: "Try it yourself and let me know if it works for you in the comments!"

4. **Example 4: Inspirational Quote or Story**
   o **What Happened**: A motivational speaker or influencer shares an inspiring story or quote with uplifting visuals.
   o **Analysis**: This Short gained traction because:
      - **Emotional Resonance**: Viewers are drawn to content that uplifts and inspires. The positive message encourages likes, shares, and comments.

- **Concise Message**: The video gets straight to the point, delivering its message clearly in a short amount of time.
- **Relatable**: Motivational content appeals to people across different demographics, making it highly shareable.
- **Call to Action**: "Share this with someone who needs a little inspiration today" motivates viewers to pass on the message.

Conclusion

Creating successful YouTube Shorts isn't just about producing great content—it's about ending with impact and encouraging viewer engagement. By using clear CTAs, asking for likes, shares, and comments, and analyzing successful Shorts to understand what works, you can increase your chances of going viral and building a dedicated following. Remember, a compelling hook, emotional resonance, and a well-crafted ending are the key ingredients to maximizing the potential of your Shorts.

IDEA 4: Visual and Audio Elements That Pop

Creating YouTube Shorts that stand out requires more than just compelling content—visuals and audio play a significant role in ensuring that your video grabs attention and keeps viewers engaged. Here's how to optimize both elements for maximum impact:

The Importance of Eye-Catching Visuals: Colors, Text, and Transitions

1. **Colors**

The colors you choose for your video can significantly influence how viewers perceive your content and whether they stop scrolling. Here's how to make your visuals pop:

- **Use Bold, Contrasting Colors**: Bright, contrasting colors grab attention, especially in the first few seconds of a video. If your video features an important message, consider using a color scheme that contrasts with the background for better visibility.
- **Maintain Consistency**: Stick to a consistent color palette throughout your videos, especially if you're building a personal brand. Using a similar color scheme will help your content feel cohesive and recognizable.

- **Color Psychology**: Different colors evoke different emotions. For instance, red can signify excitement or urgency, while blue can convey trustworthiness and calmness. Think about the emotion you want to invoke and choose your colors accordingly.

2. Text

Adding text to your Shorts can help convey your message clearly and add an extra layer of engagement. Here's how to use text effectively:

- **Keep it Short and Sweet**: Since Shorts are brief, make sure any text you add is concise and easy to read quickly. Opt for short phrases or impactful words that complement the visuals.
- **Use Bold Fonts**: Ensure your text is legible by selecting bold fonts and contrasting colors. Make sure it stands out against the background.
- **Subtitles**: Adding subtitles not only helps with accessibility but also boosts engagement, as many people watch videos without sound. It's a great way to ensure your message gets across even if the viewer is in a noisy environment.
- **Text Animations**: Dynamic text animations can help emphasize key points in your video, making the content more engaging.

3.   **Transitions**

Transitions between scenes can make your Shorts feel polished and seamless. Here's how to use transitions effectively:

- **Smooth Cuts**: Avoid awkward cuts that break the flow of your video. Use smooth transitions to move from one scene to the next, especially if you're switching locations or camera angles.
- **Keep Transitions Simple**: While transitions can add style, it's important to keep them simple and not overwhelm the viewer. Subtle fades or wipes are often more effective than flashy, complex transitions.
- **Match the Pace**: Your transitions should match the pace of your video. For fast-paced content, quick cuts and sharp transitions work well. For slower, more thoughtful content, use slower transitions to match the tone.

Selecting Music and Sound Effects: Staying Trendy and Copyright-Safe

1.   Stay   Trendy   with   Music

Music is a critical component in setting the tone and emotional pace of your Shorts. Here's how to make your audio choices work for you:

- **Use Popular Songs and Sounds**: Music that is currently trending on YouTube can give your content an extra boost. Trending songs are often picked up by the algorithm and shown to a larger audience. Look for tracks that are popular within your niche or genre.
- **Align Music with Your Message**: The music you choose should enhance the mood of your video. For example, upbeat music works well with funny or high-energy videos, while more serene tunes suit inspirational or calming content.
- **Timing is Key**: The right song or beat can heighten emotional moments in your video, but timing is everything. Make sure the music aligns with the pacing of your video to maximize its emotional impact.

2. Copyright-Safe Music

Copyright issues can be tricky, and using music without permission could result in your video being removed or demonetized. Here's how to stay safe:

- **Use YouTube's Music Library**: YouTube provides a library of free, royalty-free music and sound effects. These are safe to use in your Shorts without worrying about copyright claims.

- **Third-Party Music Services**: Platforms like Epidemic Sound, Artlist, and AudioJungle offer subscription-based libraries with a wide range of tracks that you can use legally in your content.
- **Creative Commons Music**: Some artists make their music available under Creative Commons licenses, which can be used for free, but make sure you understand the terms (some may require attribution).

3. Sound Effects

Sound effects can add an extra layer of engagement and humor to your Shorts. Here's how to use them effectively:

- **Enhance Moments**: Use sound effects to highlight key moments in your video, like adding a "pop" sound when something is revealed, or a "whoosh" when a scene changes.
- **Complement Visuals**: Make sure your sound effects match the actions happening on screen. For example, if a character jumps or moves quickly, a corresponding sound effect (like a swoosh) adds excitement.
- **Don't Overdo It**: While sound effects are fun, too many can distract from the core content. Use them sparingly to accentuate

important moments, but don't let them overpower the main audio.

Leveraging YouTube's Built-In Editing Tools Effectively

YouTube offers several built-in editing tools that can enhance your Shorts, even if you don't have advanced video editing skills. Here's how to use them to your advantage:

1.   Trimming   and   Cutting
One of the easiest ways to create a sharp, engaging Short is to cut out unnecessary content. YouTube's trimming tool allows you to remove any footage that doesn't contribute to your video's impact, ensuring it's concise and engaging.

- **Tip**: Trim your video to the most engaging moments—avoid any long intro or outro sequences that may cause viewers to lose interest.

2.   Adding   Text   and   Stickers
YouTube allows you to add text overlays and stickers to your Shorts, which can be helpful for emphasizing key points or adding some fun elements to your video.

- **Tip**: Use text sparingly—ensure it doesn't distract from the visuals but complements them. Stickers can be fun but should fit with the tone of your video.

3. Applying Filters and Effects

YouTube's effects and filters can change the overall look and feel of your video. You can adjust the brightness, contrast, and saturation to make your visuals pop, or apply filters that align with your video's mood.

- **Tip**: Keep effects subtle—too much editing can take away from the authentic, raw feel of a Short, so use filters that complement rather than overwhelm the content.

4. Music and Sound Integration

YouTube's built-in music library offers an easy way to add background music or sound effects. You can choose from a wide range of genres and moods, and even adjust the volume levels to make sure the music doesn't overpower your voice or other sounds.

- **Tip**: Ensure the music you choose doesn't clash with your content or overpower important audio cues. The goal is to support the visuals, not compete with them.

Conclusion

In YouTube Shorts, every second counts, so maximizing the impact of your visuals and audio is essential. By using eye-catching colors, dynamic text, smooth transitions, and trending, copyright-safe music, you can ensure that your content stands out. Leveraging YouTube's built-in editing tools can also simplify the process of creating polished, professional-looking Shorts, even for beginners. Focus on creating a sensory experience that captivates viewers and keeps them coming back for more!

IDEA 5: Timing Is Everything

In the world of YouTube Shorts, timing isn't just about knowing when to post—it's about understanding the rhythm of your content, how to keep it concise but complete, and how to leverage trends and timely events. Here's how to master the timing of your Shorts for maximum impact:

The Ideal Length for a Short: Keeping It Concise Yet Complete

1. Stick to the 60-Second Limit
The beauty of YouTube Shorts lies in their brevity. While YouTube allows videos up to 60 seconds, it's essential to be mindful of attention spans. Many successful Shorts are closer to 15 to 30 seconds long, delivering their content in a quick,

engaging format. Keeping your video short allows viewers to watch it multiple times and increases the likelihood of it being shared.

- **Tip**: Aim to deliver your message or entertainment in under 30 seconds for better engagement. Keep it concise, sharp, and clear.

2. No Fluff—Get to the Point
Viewers on YouTube Shorts are looking for quick entertainment, information, or inspiration. Every second counts, so avoid unnecessary filler and make sure your message is clear from the very beginning.

- **Tip**: In your opening moments, set up the hook—whether it's a question, a preview of what's to come, or something visually or emotionally compelling. Engage immediately to keep their attention.

3. Provide Value in Every Second
Even though your video is short, make sure it still feels complete. Don't leave your audience hanging. Whether it's a laugh, a takeaway, or a satisfying conclusion, aim to provide value in every second.

- **Tip**: For tutorial or informational Shorts, even if the time is short, make sure the viewer comes away with something useful or memorable, like a quick hack or a key insight.

Posting Schedules: When to Upload for Maximum Visibility

The timing of when you post your Shorts can impact how many people see them. Here's how to make sure you're posting at the optimal times:

1. Know Your Audience's Active Hours To maximize visibility, post when your target audience is most likely to be online. YouTube's algorithm takes into account engagement, so if your video gets initial traction, it's more likely to be promoted. Knowing when your followers are active is essential.

- **Tip**: You can track when your viewers are most active by using YouTube Analytics. Look at the "When Your Viewers Are on YouTube" section to get a sense of peak times.

2. Experiment with Different Times While there are general best practices for posting times, such as late mornings or early evenings, the optimal time may vary based on your audience's demographic. Experiment with posting at different times of day, and track how your videos perform.

- **Tip**: Test posting at different hours across several days of the week, then analyze the performance using YouTube Analytics. This will help you find patterns specific to your audience.

3. Consistency Is Key

Posting consistently can help build momentum for your channel. Even if the exact timing isn't always perfect, regular uploads increase your chances of being noticed. Create a schedule that you can stick to, and try to upload new Shorts on the same days or times each week.

- **Tip**: Consistency doesn't mean posting multiple times a day—two to three times a week is a good starting point. This keeps your audience engaged without overwhelming them.

4. Peak Times on YouTube

Based on general trends, YouTube's peak traffic times are typically between **2 PM and 4 PM on weekdays** (local time), as well as **weekends around noon to 6 PM**. Posting during these times can give your Shorts a better chance of being discovered.

- **Tip**: If your audience is international, adjust your posting schedule to account for time zone differences.

Capitalizing on Trends and Timely Content

1.   Stay   on   Top   of   Trends
Trends are the lifeblood of YouTube Shorts. Trending challenges, songs, memes, and popular topics are perfect opportunities to gain traction quickly. Jumping on these trends can help your Shorts get more visibility, as the YouTube algorithm tends to push out content that aligns with trending topics.

- **Tip**: Use the "Explore" tab on YouTube to stay up to date on trending content. If you spot a trend you can tie into your niche, jump on it quickly to capitalize on the wave of interest.

2. Create Timely Content Around Events
Timely content related to holidays, breaking news, or seasonal events can give your Shorts an edge. Whether it's creating something fun for a holiday or commenting on current events, timely content is more likely to be shared and engaged with, especially if it's well-timed and well-executed.

- **Tip**: If there's a major event or trend (like a viral moment in pop culture), create a Short that ties into it. For instance, during the Super Bowl or major film releases, consider creating themed content to attract viewers interested in that event.

3. Use Hashtags for Discoverability

Hashtags play a vital role in helping your Shorts reach the right audience. Be strategic about using popular and relevant hashtags, especially those related to trending topics, events, or challenges. But avoid using too many unrelated hashtags, as this can come off as spammy.

- **Tip**: Use a mix of broad hashtags (e.g., #funny, #lifehacks) and niche-specific hashtags to increase discoverability. If a hashtag is trending or tied to an event (e.g., #WorldCup or #NewYear2025), incorporate that into your post.

4. Ride the Wave of Trending Audio

Music and sound effects are integral to YouTube Shorts, and using trending audio can give your videos an automatic boost. YouTube often promotes videos that use popular or trending audio clips, helping them reach a wider audience.

- **Tip**: Search for trending audio in YouTube's music library or browse through the Shorts feed to see which audio clips are currently popular. Be quick to incorporate trending sounds before they become oversaturated.

5. Leverage User-Generated Content (UGC) Trends

User-generated content is one of the most

engaging types of content on YouTube Shorts. Participate in challenges, reactions, or compilations that encourage viewers to interact and participate.

- **Tip**: Create a challenge or join an existing trend, encouraging your viewers to make their own videos and tag your channel. This not only builds engagement but also helps spread your content to a wider audience.

Conclusion

Mastering the timing of your YouTube Shorts— whether it's the length of your video, the optimal time to post, or jumping on trends—can dramatically increase your chances of success. Keep your videos concise and engaging, post regularly at strategic times, and stay ahead of trends to maintain visibility. Capitalizing on timely events and trends is your ticket to staying relevant and reaching a wider audience. Timing truly is everything, and when you get it right, your content will not only be seen but shared and appreciated across the platform.

IDEA 6: Getting Likes Through Engagement

In the world of YouTube Shorts, engagement is key to gaining visibility, growing your audience, and driving more likes. While creating compelling content is essential, your ability to prompt interaction from viewers is what will truly help you succeed. This chapter will explore effective ways to encourage likes through strategic engagement.

Crafting Calls-to-Action (CTAs) That Work

A call-to-action (CTA) is a simple, direct instruction that tells your viewers what to do next. For YouTube Shorts, a strong CTA can lead to increased engagement, including likes, shares, and comments. Here's how to craft CTAs that work:

1.   Be   Clear   and   Direct
Your CTA should be easy to understand and encourage action immediately after the viewer finishes watching. Whether it's asking viewers to like, comment, or share, be direct and to the point.

- **Example**: "If you enjoyed this, hit that like button!" or "Tag a friend who needs to see this!"

2. Ask for Engagement in the Form of a Question

One of the most effective CTAs is asking a question related to your video. This invites viewers to leave comments, which can boost engagement and interaction.

- **Example**: "What do you think? Let me know in the comments!" or "What would you do in this situation?"

3. Use Action-Oriented Language

Encourage viewers to take immediate action by using action verbs such as "like," "comment," "share," "subscribe," or "watch more."

- **Example**: "Like this video for more tips!" or "Comment your favorite moment below!"

4. Make CTAs Fun and Interactive

If your audience feels like they're part of something fun or engaging, they'll be more likely to act. Try to incorporate a sense of excitement or curiosity into your CTA.

- **Example**: "Hit the thumbs up if you agree!" or "Share this with a friend who needs a laugh!"

5. Provide a Sense of Urgency

Creating a sense of urgency in your CTA can make viewers feel like they need to act immediately. This can be especially effective when used in limited-time offers or trend-related content.

- **Example**: "Like now before time runs out!" or "Hurry, comment your answer before the video ends!"

Encouraging Comments and Replies to Drive Algorithm Engagement

YouTube's algorithm places significant weight on comments as a form of engagement, so encouraging your viewers to comment is crucial for gaining traction. Here's how to get your audience talking:

1.   Ask   Thought-Provoking   Questions
Asking questions in your videos—especially ones that spark curiosity or invite opinions—encourages viewers to comment their thoughts. It can be as simple as asking for their opinion or getting them to share their experiences.

- **Example**: "What's your favorite life hack? Let's talk about it in the comments!" or "Have you ever tried this? How did it go for you?"

2.   Reply   to   Comments
Engage with your audience by replying to their comments. This not only encourages more people to comment (as they'll see you're active), but it

also builds a relationship with your viewers, making them more likely to engage with your future content.

- **Tip**: Make it a habit to reply to comments, especially when viewers ask questions or share personal experiences. Your active participation encourages others to comment as well.

3. Host a Challenge or Poll

Challenges or polls are a great way to encourage viewers to share their thoughts and opinions. By making the comment section a place for people to participate in something fun, you can drive up engagement.

- **Example**: "I challenge you to try this and let me know how it goes!" or "What's your favorite ice cream flavor? Let's settle the debate in the comments!"

4. Highlight Comments in Your Videos

If a viewer leaves a thoughtful or entertaining comment, consider featuring it in your next video. This encourages others to comment as well, knowing they might get recognition.

- **Example**: "Shoutout to [user] for this amazing tip! Keep the suggestions coming!"

Leveraging Pinned Comments and Hashtags

Using pinned comments and hashtags can be a powerful way to further encourage engagement and boost your video's visibility. Here's how you can use these features effectively:

1. Pinning Comments to Drive Engagement
Pinning a comment to the top of your video's comment section allows you to highlight a specific message. This could be a CTA, a question you want viewers to answer, or simply a thank-you message for watching.

- **Tip**: Pin your CTA or a question to encourage more comments. For example, "What do you think about this? Drop your thoughts below, and I'll reply to as many as I can!"

2. Creating a Community with Pinned Comments
You can use pinned comments to build a community feel by acknowledging your audience or encouraging further interaction. This helps create a sense of inclusivity and prompts viewers to engage.

- **Example**: "Thanks for watching! I'd love to hear how you're tackling this challenge—share in the comments!"

3. Hashtags for Better Discoverability
Hashtags not only categorize your content but

also make it more discoverable. By including relevant hashtags in your title or description, you increase the chances of your Shorts reaching a broader audience.

- **Tip**: Use popular, relevant hashtags to boost discoverability (e.g., #funny, #lifehacks, #DIY). Avoid overusing them, though—keep it to 2-3 key hashtags.

4.   Trend-Specific   Hashtags
Using trending hashtags can help your content reach the right audience. These hashtags often come with challenges or viral topics, giving your Shorts an opportunity to join the wider conversation and gain exposure.

- **Example**: If there's a viral meme or trend, use the specific hashtag (#ViralChallenge2025 or #NewYearNewMe) to join the discussion.

Conclusion

Engagement is the driving force behind the success of your YouTube Shorts. Crafting effective CTAs, encouraging comments, and leveraging pinned comments and hashtags are powerful tools that can significantly boost your visibility and likes. By creating a cycle of engagement—where viewers feel invited to interact, share, and comment—you not only foster community but also increase your chances of algorithmic promotion. Keep engaging with your audience, and they'll reward you with more likes, shares, and comments.

IDEA 7: Leveraging Analytics

Analytics are the backbone of content strategy, especially when it comes to refining and improving your YouTube Shorts. By understanding and utilizing YouTube's analytics, you can make data-driven decisions that will help you optimize your videos, grow your audience, and increase engagement. In this chapter, we'll explore how to use YouTube's analytics dashboard effectively, identify key metrics to track, and use the data to enhance your Shorts.

Understanding YouTube's Analytics Dashboard

YouTube's analytics dashboard provides a wealth of information about your channel's performance. To access it, simply go to your YouTube Studio and click on the "Analytics" tab. Here, you'll find detailed insights about your content, audience, and how your videos are performing across different metrics.

The dashboard is divided into several key sections:

- **Overview**: This section gives you a high-level snapshot of how your channel is performing, including the total number of views, watch time, and subscriber count.
- **Reach**: This tab shows how viewers are discovering your Shorts, including impressions (how many times your video was shown to users) and click-through rate (CTR).
- **Engagement**: Here, you can see how long viewers are watching your videos, which videos are the most engaging, and where viewers are dropping off.
- **Audience**: This section reveals insights into who is watching your videos, including demographics, locations, and when they are most likely to be online.

By understanding these sections, you can dig deeper into what's working and what isn't, allowing you to refine your content strategy for greater success.

Key Metrics to Track: Views, Watch Time, and Engagement Rate

When analyzing your YouTube Shorts, there are three primary metrics you should focus on to measure the success of your videos:

1. Views

The number of views a video receives indicates how many people have watched it. However, views alone don't tell the full story. The real value of views lies in how they correlate with your engagement and overall growth.

- **What to do with this metric**: Track which videos get the most views and try to identify patterns—are there specific topics, styles, or formats that seem to perform better?

2. Watch Time

Watch time refers to the total minutes viewers have spent watching your video. Unlike views, which are simply a count of how many times your video has been viewed, watch time gives you an understanding of how engaged viewers are with your content.

- **What to do with this metric**: YouTube's algorithm prioritizes videos with higher watch time, so if a particular Short has a higher watch time, it's likely being promoted more. Pay attention to the videos with the most watch time and analyze their content to replicate successful elements.

3. Engagement Rate

Engagement includes likes, comments, shares, and other interactions that indicate how involved your audience is with your content. Engagement rate is the percentage of viewers who interact with your video relative to the total number of views.

- **What to do with this metric**: High engagement rates are a positive signal to YouTube's algorithm that your video is compelling. Track which types of calls-to-action or content prompts encourage the most interaction, and consider incorporating those tactics into future Shorts.

Using Data to Refine and Improve Your Shorts

Once you understand these key metrics, it's time to put the data to work. Here's how you can use analytics to continuously refine and improve your YouTube Shorts:

1. Identify Patterns in Popular Content

Look for patterns in the types of content that perform well. For example, do certain topics consistently get more views or higher engagement? Is there a specific format (e.g., tutorials, challenges, humor) that resonates more with your audience?

- **Action**: Use this information to double down on what's working. If your humorous content tends to get more views, consider creating more lighthearted, funny Shorts. If educational content gets more engagement, create more instructional or informative videos.

2. Optimize Video Length Based on Watch Time

Watch time data reveals how long people are sticking around to watch your videos. If your Shorts tend to lose viewers before the end, it could mean they're too long, or the content doesn't maintain viewer interest.

- **Action**: Experiment with different video lengths and analyze the results. Aim to create Shorts that are both concise and captivating, keeping the audience engaged for as long as possible.

3. Refine Your Thumbnails, Titles, and Descriptions

The reach tab of your analytics will show you the click-through rate (CTR) of your videos. A low CTR may suggest that your thumbnail or title isn't compelling enough to encourage viewers to click on the video.

- **Action**: Test different thumbnails, titles, and descriptions to see what garners more attention. Keep your thumbnails visually appealing and relevant to the video, and ensure your title is concise but intriguing.

4. Adjust Posting Schedule

The audience section of your analytics shows when your viewers are most active. By posting during peak times, you maximize the chances of your video being seen by more people.

- **Action**: Experiment with different posting times and track the results. Once you identify the optimal posting schedule, stick to it for consistency.

5. Monitor Audience Retention

The engagement tab provides insights into how well viewers are sticking with your videos. If your retention rate drops significantly during a certain part of your video, that could be a sign that your content isn't holding their attention.

- **Action**: Look for trends in where people drop off and try to identify why. It could be that your intro is too long or your hook isn't strong enough. Make adjustments to keep viewers engaged from start to finish.

6. A/B Test and Iterate

YouTube provides valuable data, but sometimes, testing different strategies is the best way to find what works. Create variations of your Shorts—whether it's the length, format, or approach—and track how they perform to see which one has the most success.

- **Action**: Test different types of CTAs, visuals, or storytelling approaches to see which gets more likes and engagement. Continuous iteration will help you hone your craft.

Conclusion

Leveraging analytics is an essential part of mastering YouTube Shorts. By tracking key metrics such as views, watch time, and engagement rate, you can refine your content strategy, identify what resonates with your audience, and continuously improve your Shorts. Don't simply rely on gut instinct—let data guide your decisions, experiment with different strategies, and watch as your content grows in both quality and reach. With the right analytics insights, you can increase your chances of getting more likes and boosting your presence on YouTube.

IDEA 8: Monetizing Your Shorts

Monetizing YouTube Shorts is an exciting way to turn your creative efforts into a steady income stream. With YouTube's growing emphasis on short-form content, creators now have more opportunities to make money from their Shorts. In this chapter, we'll explore how likes contribute to monetization, how to partner with brands for sponsored Shorts, and how to drive traffic to other revenue streams like merchandise and online courses.

How Likes Contribute to Your Channel's Monetization

Likes are one of the primary indicators of engagement on YouTube Shorts. The more likes your videos receive, the more likely your content is to be recommended by YouTube's algorithm, which can increase visibility and audience growth. But beyond the algorithmic benefits, likes also play a role in monetization, particularly when it comes to ad revenue and the YouTube Partner Program (YPP).

1. YouTube Partner Program (YPP)

To qualify for the YouTube Partner Program and start earning ad revenue, you must meet specific eligibility requirements:

- 1,000 subscribers
- 4,000 watch hours in the last 12 months (or 10 million Shorts views in 90 days for Shorts monetization)

When your videos get a lot of likes, it's an indicator that viewers are engaged and enjoying your content. High engagement, including likes, can help you hit these thresholds more quickly, especially if your Shorts are being recommended to new viewers through the algorithm.

- **Action**: Focus on creating content that garners likes and engagement. Consistently getting likes on your Shorts will increase your chances of meeting YouTube's monetization requirements, especially if your content goes viral and attracts a broad audience.

2. Super Thanks (For Engagement)

Super Thanks is a feature that allows viewers to give monetary support to your videos directly. While this feature is not exclusive to Shorts, it can be particularly effective if your Shorts are getting significant likes and comments.

- **Action**: Once you're eligible for monetization, enable Super Thanks on your videos to allow your audience to show appreciation and support for your work. Engaging with your community through comments and CTAs (like "Thanks for the love!" or "Consider supporting this channel through Super Thanks") can help generate donations from your most loyal fans.

Partnering with Brands for Sponsored Shorts

Brand partnerships are one of the most lucrative ways to monetize YouTube Shorts. Brands are eager to connect with the younger, engaged audience that Shorts attract, and they often look for influencers with substantial reach and a strong connection to their viewers. Here's how you can start partnering with brands:

1. Build Your Brand and Niche

Before you can approach brands for sponsorships, it's essential to establish a niche and a personal brand that resonates with your audience. Whether you're focusing on fashion, technology, fitness, or entertainment, having a clear niche will help you attract brands that align with your content.

- **Action**: Identify your audience demographics, interests, and values. Make sure your content aligns with a particular brand's target market to increase the likelihood of brand collaboration.

2. Create High-Quality Content That Aligns with Brands

Brands want to see that your content is not only engaging but also authentic. When creating sponsored Shorts, your content should seamlessly integrate the brand's product or message in a way that feels natural to your audience.

- **Action**: Be transparent about sponsorships. Viewers appreciate honesty, so always disclose when content is sponsored. Craft your Shorts to highlight the product or service in a way that adds value to the viewer, rather than appearing overly promotional.

3. Reach Out to Brands and Agencies

Once you've established yourself as a creator, start reaching out to brands, influencers' agencies, or platforms like GrapeVine or Channel Pages to find opportunities for sponsored content. Ensure your pitch is professional and highlights your audience demographics, engagement rates, and how you align with the brand's goals.

- **Action**: Prepare a media kit with your channel statistics (views, engagement rates, audience demographics) and send it to potential brands or marketing agencies.

4. Negotiate the Terms

When working with a brand, negotiate a deal that reflects the value of your platform. Sponsored content can be lucrative, so ensure you're fairly compensated for your work. This may involve direct payments, free products, or other benefits.

- **Action**: Understand the value of your content and don't be afraid to negotiate. You can set rates based on your reach and the type of collaboration you're offering (e.g., a dedicated sponsored Short, product placements, etc.).

Driving Traffic to Other Revenue Streams (Merchandise, Courses, etc.)

While monetizing your Shorts through ads and sponsorships is great, there are also other ways to generate revenue outside of YouTube. By leveraging your Shorts to drive traffic to other revenue-generating platforms, you can maximize your earnings.

1. Promote Merchandise

If you have your own merchandise (T-shirts, hoodies, hats, etc.), YouTube Shorts can serve as a fantastic promotional tool. Use your videos to showcase your products in a fun and engaging way, incorporating them into the content where possible.

- **Action**: Create a Shorts series around your merchandise, showing off different products or using your merchandise in fun, relatable situations. You can add a link to your merchandise in the description or even use YouTube's merchandise shelf (if eligible).

2. Drive Traffic to Online Courses or Services

If you offer an online course, coaching service, or other digital products, Shorts are an excellent way to drive traffic to those offerings. By providing free valuable content in your Shorts, you can create curiosity and incentivize viewers to check out your full offering.

- **Action**: Create Shorts that provide snippets of your courses or services and encourage viewers to visit your website or landing page for more information. Use CTAs like "Want to learn more? Check out my course in the link below!" to drive traffic.

3. Affiliate Marketing

Affiliate marketing allows you to earn a commission by promoting other people's products or services. By recommending tools, software, or other products that align with your audience's interests, you can make money through affiliate links.

- **Action**: Integrate affiliate marketing into your Shorts by promoting products that complement your content. For example, if you create cooking content, include affiliate links to kitchen gadgets in the description.

Conclusion

Monetizing YouTube Shorts is a fantastic way to turn your creativity into income. By focusing on getting likes and engagement, partnering with brands for sponsorships, and driving traffic to other revenue streams, you can build a sustainable and profitable channel. Keep refining your approach, analyzing your audience's behavior, and exploring different monetization opportunities, and you'll be well on your way to turning your passion for creating Shorts into a full-fledged business.

IDEA 9: Overcoming Challenges

Creating successful YouTube Shorts is not without its challenges. While the platform offers incredible opportunities, content creators often face low engagement, burnout, and intense competition. This chapter will address these common obstacles and offer strategies to help you navigate them and keep growing your channel.

Dealing with Low Engagement and Dislikes

Low engagement and dislikes are common experiences for many YouTube creators, especially when you're just starting. While it can be disheartening, it's important to view these as opportunities for growth rather than setbacks. Here's how to handle them:

1. Understand Why Engagement is Low

If your Shorts aren't getting the engagement you expect, take a step back and analyze your content. Ask yourself the following questions:

- Are you capturing attention in the first few seconds?
- Is your content providing value to your target audience (entertainment, education, inspiration)?

- Are you consistently posting content?

Sometimes low engagement is simply a result of not hitting the right audience or having a mismatch between your content and what people are looking for. Be open to experimenting and tweaking your approach.

- **Action**: Use YouTube analytics to track where viewers drop off in your videos and adjust your content accordingly. Look for patterns that can help you improve future Shorts.

2. Addressing Dislikes Constructively

Dislikes are part of being a content creator and shouldn't deter you. Instead of focusing on negative feedback, use it as an opportunity for constructive criticism. Dislikes often reflect personal preferences, but they can also signal that you need to adjust your content for better engagement.

- **Action**: Consider asking for feedback directly from your audience in the comments or through polls. Address any legitimate concerns or suggestions in future videos. Over time, you'll learn what resonates with your viewers and what doesn't.

3. Stay Positive and Don't Let Negativity Affect You

One of the hardest parts of content creation is managing negative comments or dislikes, especially when you put a lot of effort into your work. Remember, it's natural to encounter criticism, but don't let it discourage you from continuing to create.

- **Action**: Focus on the positive aspects of content creation, such as viewer appreciation and personal growth. Surround yourself with a supportive community and remind yourself of your long-term goals.

Staying Consistent While Avoiding Burnout

Consistency is key to building an audience on YouTube Shorts, but it can also lead to burnout if you're not careful. Here's how to stay on track without sacrificing your mental and physical well-being.

1. Set Realistic Goals

When you're trying to grow a channel, it's easy to fall into the trap of posting multiple times a day or week. However, this level of commitment can quickly lead to burnout. Instead, focus on setting realistic, achievable goals for your posting schedule.

- **Action**: Start with a manageable schedule, such as posting 2-3 Shorts a week. As you grow more comfortable with your process, you can increase your posting frequency. Focus on quality over quantity to maintain consistency without overwhelming yourself.

2. Batch Your Content Creation

Batching content creation is a great way to stay ahead and reduce the pressure to constantly create new videos. Set aside a dedicated time to shoot multiple Shorts in one go, so you have content ready to go for the upcoming days or weeks.

- **Action**: Create a content calendar and batch your Shorts production during a single session. This allows you to focus on creating without the constant worry of having to film new content each day.

3. Take Breaks and Rest

Rest is crucial for creativity and long-term success. Burnout can diminish the quality of your work, leading to lower engagement and a lack of motivation. Make sure to take regular breaks from content creation to recharge.

- **Action**: Plan time away from creating content, whether it's a weekend off or a short vacation. Use this time to relax, find new inspiration, or simply recharge your creative energy.

4. Delegate Tasks if Possible

As your channel grows, consider outsourcing certain tasks like video editing, thumbnail design, or social media management. This can free up more time for you to focus on creating content and maintaining your well-being.

- **Action**: Hire a freelancer or use tools that automate tasks (e.g., scheduling posts, editing templates). This can help you maintain a steady output of content without burning out.

Handling Competition and Staying Unique

The world of YouTube Shorts is highly competitive, with countless creators vying for the attention of the same audience. In this environment, it's important to differentiate yourself and stay authentic.

1. Analyze Competitors, But Don't Copy

Looking at what your competitors are doing can be a useful learning tool, but avoid simply copying their content. Instead, use their strategies as inspiration to find what works for you.

- **Action**: Analyze popular Shorts in your niche and identify trends. What are the common elements? What can you do differently? Find a way to put your unique spin on those ideas to stand out from the crowd.

2. Stay True to Your Voice and Niche

The best way to differentiate yourself is by being authentic. Focus on creating content that reflects your personal style and interests, and don't try to imitate someone else's success.

- **Action**: Be transparent about your personality, values, and interests. Create Shorts that showcase your unique voice and cater to your specific audience's needs.

3. Adapt to Change Without Losing Your Identity

Trends on YouTube change rapidly, but you don't have to chase every trend. It's important to stay flexible and adapt your content to current trends, but without losing your unique identity.

- **Action**: Pick trends that align with your style and incorporate them into your content in a way that still feels authentic. This balance of flexibility and consistency will help you stay relevant without losing what makes you stand out.

4. Collaborate with Other Creators

Collaboration is a great way to expand your reach while staying true to your own brand. By collaborating with other creators in your niche, you can tap into their audiences and introduce them to your content.

- **Action**: Reach out to other YouTubers with similar interests for collaborative Shorts. Cross-promotion can be mutually beneficial and help you stand out in a crowded space.

Conclusion

Overcoming challenges is part of the journey of content creation. Dealing with low engagement, avoiding burnout, and handling competition are hurdles every YouTuber faces, but with the right mindset and strategies, you can overcome them. Stay focused on your goals, maintain your uniqueness, and prioritize your well-being as you continue to grow your channel. By doing so, you'll be better equipped to thrive in the dynamic world of YouTube Shorts.

IDEA 10: The Future of YouTube Shorts

As the digital landscape continues to evolve, YouTube Shorts is quickly becoming a dominant force in content creation. With rapid growth in viewership and engagement, the future of Shorts is bright, but it will also bring new challenges and opportunities. This chapter explores emerging trends, potential algorithm changes, and strategies for staying ahead of the curve.

Emerging Trends in Short-Form Video Content

The rise of YouTube Shorts is part of a larger trend of short-form video content, which is rapidly reshaping the way we consume media. Several key trends are expected to continue and even accelerate, creating new opportunities for creators.

1. Vertical Video Will Continue to Dominate

With mobile consumption at an all-time high, vertical videos have become the preferred format for quick and accessible content. As audiences become more accustomed to viewing content on their phones, vertical videos will likely continue to thrive. Shorts, being designed specifically for mobile viewing, will remain a key format for creators.

- **Action**: Focus on creating content that looks good in a vertical format, maximizing the screen real estate and ensuring your visuals are optimized for mobile devices.

2. Interactive and Immersive Content

As YouTube and other platforms experiment with immersive technologies like augmented reality (AR) and virtual reality (VR), short-form content may become more interactive. Imagine viewers being able to engage with a Short through interactive elements or even participating in a virtual environment.

- **Action**: Stay on the lookout for new tools or features that allow for interactive content. Incorporating AR filters, polls, or gamified elements could set your Shorts apart from others.

3. Niche Communities and Micro-Content

As short-form video continues to grow, there will be a rise in the demand for highly niche content. Smaller, highly engaged communities will form around specific interests, from DIY tutorials to deep dives into specific subcultures. These micro-communities will look for content that speaks directly to their passions and needs.

- **Action**: Identify and engage with niche communities relevant to your content. Tailor your Shorts to meet the unique needs and interests of these audiences to build loyal followers.

4. User-Generated Content and Challenges

User-generated content (UGC) is already a major part of YouTube Shorts, but as the format continues to evolve, we'll likely see more brands and creators encouraging challenges and collaborations. These challenges allow viewers to participate and create their own content, furthering engagement and interaction.

- **Action**: Consider starting your own challenge or hashtag to encourage viewer participation. Tap into trending challenges to gain visibility while keeping your content authentic and fun.

Preparing for Algorithm Changes and New Features

The YouTube algorithm is constantly evolving to prioritize new content and improve user experience. As YouTube Shorts becomes more integrated into the platform, the algorithm will adapt to enhance its performance, making it essential for creators to stay updated on any changes that may impact their reach.

1. Understanding Algorithm Updates

The YouTube algorithm is designed to recommend videos that keep users engaged for longer periods. While Shorts content is brief, it's crucial that your videos capture attention immediately and keep viewers watching until the end. Future algorithm updates may focus on improving engagement metrics, like watch time or interactions (likes, comments, shares).

- **Action**: Monitor any updates to YouTube's algorithm by keeping up with news from YouTube creators, forums, and official announcements. Adapt your strategy based on these changes to ensure your Shorts stay visible.

2. Utilizing New Features

YouTube is constantly adding new features to Shorts, from new editing tools to collaborations with other platforms. These new features can enhance your content creation process and help you stand out from the competition.

- **Action**: Stay curious and explore new features as they roll out. Experiment with new tools and use them creatively in your Shorts to keep your content fresh and relevant.

3. AI and Personalization

As AI continues to improve, YouTube may implement even more advanced personalization algorithms, allowing for hyper-targeted recommendations based on individual user behavior. This could create opportunities for content creators to reach even more engaged viewers.

- **Action**: Ensure that your content is aligned with your audience's preferences. Use YouTube Analytics to gain insights into what resonates with your viewers and tailor your content accordingly.

Tips for Staying Ahead of the Curve

The digital landscape is fast-paced, and the key to success on YouTube Shorts will be adaptability. Here are some tips for staying ahead of the curve as new trends and features emerge.

1. Keep Experimenting with Content Formats

Short-form content is constantly evolving. To stay ahead, continually experiment with different video formats, from tutorials to behind-the-scenes clips, and see what resonates with your audience. Adapt your content to current trends without losing your unique voice.

- **Action**: Regularly assess the performance of your Shorts and experiment with new ideas and formats. Stay flexible and open to trying new approaches as the platform evolves.

2. Engage with Your Audience in Real-Time

Real-time engagement is a great way to stay connected with your audience. Live Q&A sessions, real-time reactions to trending topics, or interactive polls can create a sense of community and keep viewers coming back for more.

- **Action**: Use YouTube's live features or engage with your audience through comments and polls. Directly respond to your audience's feedback to build loyalty and encourage more engagement.

3. Collaborate with Other Creators

The future of YouTube Shorts is about collaboration. Working with other creators can help you tap into new audiences and grow your influence. Collaboration fosters community-building and cross-promotion, which is vital for success on the platform.

- **Action**: Reach out to creators in your niche for collaborative Shorts. Cross-promote each other's channels to share audiences and build a supportive community of creators.

4. Stay Informed About Industry Trends

YouTube Shorts is not the only short-form video platform vying for attention. Platforms like TikTok, Instagram Reels, and Snapchat are also in the game. Stay informed about trends across these platforms, as they often influence one another.

- **Action**: Follow industry news, attend webinars, and participate in online communities to stay informed about what's happening in the world of short-form video content.

The future of YouTube Shorts is bright and full of potential. By staying ahead of emerging trends, adapting to changes in the algorithm, and utilizing new features, you can continue to grow your channel and build a lasting presence in the short-form video landscape. Embrace the future with curiosity, creativity, and flexibility, and you'll be well-positioned for success in the ever-evolving world of YouTube Shorts.

Conclusion

As we wrap up this guide, let's take a moment to reflect on the key strategies that will help you succeed in getting likes on YouTube Shorts and growing your channel in the process. Short-form video content is more than just a trend—it's a powerful tool for creators to build a loyal audience and make a lasting impact in the digital space.

Recap of the Key Strategies for Getting Likes on YouTube Shorts

1. **Crafting Engaging Content**: Start with a strong 3-second hook to capture attention immediately. Create content that resonates emotionally—whether through humor, surprise, or inspiration. Build a narrative within those precious seconds to keep viewers hooked until the end.
2. **Leveraging Visuals and Audio**: Ensure that your visuals pop with vibrant colors, smooth transitions, and attention-grabbing text. Select trendy, copyright-safe music and sound effects to enhance your Shorts' impact, and use YouTube's built-in editing tools to add a professional touch.
3. **Optimizing Timing**: Keep your Shorts concise yet impactful, focusing on delivering value quickly. Experiment with

posting times and stay ahead of trends to capitalize on what's currently popular.

4. **Driving Engagement**: Craft compelling calls-to-action (CTAs) that encourage likes, shares, and comments. Foster a sense of community by interacting with your audience, replying to comments, and leveraging hashtags and pinned comments to increase visibility.

5. **Using Analytics to Improve**: Regularly check your YouTube Analytics to track views, watch time, and engagement rates. Use this data to refine your content strategy and improve performance over time.

6. **Monetizing and Staying Consistent**: Build monetization opportunities through likes, sponsorships, and promoting other revenue streams. Remain consistent, and even when facing challenges like low engagement or burnout, keep pushing forward.

Motivational Insights for Aspiring Creators

The path to success on YouTube Shorts is not always linear, but it's within reach for anyone willing to put in the effort. Whether you're just starting or are already experimenting with content, remember that every great creator began with one video. Don't be afraid to take risks, experiment with new ideas, and embrace feedback from your audience.

The journey to mastering Shorts takes persistence, creativity, and adaptability. As the digital world continues to evolve, so will your approach. Keep learning, growing, and innovating—each like, comment, and share is a small victory on the road to bigger successes.

Encouragement to Start Experimenting with the Formula

Now is the time to put everything you've learned into action. Start experimenting with the formula, apply the strategies discussed, and track your results. Your unique voice, creativity, and authenticity are what will set you apart from the crowd. There's no one-size-fits-all approach to success—only the one that fits your content and audience best.

Get ready to create, share, and engage. The world of YouTube Shorts is waiting for your voice. The next like could be the start of something big!

Good luck, and happy creating!

www.ingramcontent.com/pod-product-compliance
Lightning Source LLC
LaVergne TN
LVHW052311060326
832902LV00021B/3829